Clumber Spaniel Dog As Pet

The Best Pet Owner Manual
On Clumber Spaniel Dog
Care, Training, Personality,
Grooming, Feeding And
Health For Beginners

GW00468154

Adam Kelly

Table of Contents

CHAPTER ONE

Clumber Spaniel

The biggest of all spaniels, the Clumber Spaniel is a canine fit for a ruler. Also, to be sure, a large part of the variety's initial history bases on French and British respectability.

Reproduced to be a gundog that represents considerable authority in hunting in weighty cover, the Clumber Spaniel has the long, delicate coat normal for all spaniels. Most Clumbers are white in shading, while a few examples show brown, lemon or orange markings. It is reasonably intensely fabricated canine with substantial bone construction and a gigantic head. This enormous gag empowers the Clumber Spaniel to recover a wide range of game. The Clumbers have 'liquefying' heads and their faces take on a sluggish, sorrowful demeanor.

Albeit not quite so quick as most different types of spaniels, the Clumber has incredible endurance and can jog along at a sluggish walk for a really long time. It is additionally an exceptionally smart canine equipped for autonomous reasoning. These attributes make it a magnificent hunting canine; an assignment the variety was utilized for noticeably among the British nobility. They are likewise delicate and adoring and make superb pets too.

Beginning

In spite of the fact that their precise history is hazy, it is generally accepted that Clumber Spaniels began from the weapon canines reared by the French honorability in the mid 1600s. One hypothesis of beginning goes onto express that the French Duc de

Noailles, under danger from the French Revolution, parted with his valued pet hotel of hunting canines to the Duke of Newcastle at Clumber Park. It is accepted that the variety was created and culminated here by the Duke's gamekeeper William Mansel. Notwithstanding, it is sure that the variety gets its name from Clumber Park.

The variety delighted in extraordinary support from different British Royals, including Queen Victoria's partner Prince Albert and his child King Edward VII. Sovereign Victoria specifies the variety in her journal as follows:

"Left straightforwardly after breakfast before Albert went to shoot. He had his 7 fine Clumber Spaniels with us and we went into the Slopes, with such an interesting old Gamekeeper, Walters, all together that I should perceive how the canines discovered their game. They are such dear, pleasant canines."

The reproducing of Clumber Spaniels was confined to British honorability up until the mid nineteenth century, and was stopped totally during World War I. This made their numbers drop definitely and it took the endeavors of King George V to restore the variety.

Family

It is accepted that the Clumber Spaniel's family incorporates blood from the now terminated Alpine Spaniel, the Basset Hound and the St. Bernard.

CHAPTER TWO

Future and Size

Tragically, this variety has an assortment of medical problems, some of which abbreviate their life expectancy. Most Clumbers live somewhere in the range of 10 and 12 years.

These are medium size canines, standing 17 to 20 pounds and tipping the scales at a powerful 55 to 85 pounds.

Defensive Ability

This variety isn't known for its nibble or its bark. Most Clumbers range from amicable to saved with outsiders. They are an especially tranquil variety and don't view their obligations as a guard dog extremely in a serious way.

Energy Level

At the point when youthful, these spaniels are pretty much as wild as some other. In any case, as they age, they will more often than not relax.

All Clumber Spaniels are genuinely competent. All things considered, they were reproduced to be powerful trackers. A few grown-ups may should be persuaded to work out, which is indispensable to keeping them fit and solid. This variety has a back vulnerable to injury. Muscle tone can assist with staying away from issues.

Preparing

Clumber Spaniels are dedicated, smart canines and are anxious to please. In this way best support methods work magnificently with the variety. They can be prepared to chase and recover game without any problem.

CHAPTER THREE

Weight

Clumber Spaniel guys range in weight from 70-85 pounds.

Demeanor and Behavior

Clumber Spaniels are viewed as one of the more laid-back types of spaniels and have delicate, accommodating dispositions. They are anyway profoundly shrewd and autonomous, and may turn stiff-necked when not given legitimate initiative. Like most savvy working varieties, Clumber

Spaniels react well to the initiative of quiet, decisive proprietors.

Clumber Spaniels are perky and coexist superbly with youngsters. They likewise exist together calmly with different canines and different creatures. They can anyway be unapproachable with outsiders and endeavors ought to be taken to mingle them almost immediately throughout everyday life.

These canines are not barkers and don't make great watchman canines.

Normal Health Problems

Clumber Spaniels are a for the most part solid variety of canine. Be that as it may, they are inclined to illnesses, for example, hip dysplasia elbow dysplasia, hypothyroidism and von Willebrand's sickness.

Future

A very actually liked Clumber Spaniel will partake in a life expectancy of 10-12 years.

CHAPTER FOUR

Exercise Requirements

Clumber Spaniel young doggies are exceptionally perky and have a lot of energy. They anyway delayed down altogether as they age and aren't extremely dynamic as grown-ups. This makes them inadmissible for dynamic, athletic proprietors that appreciate running and climbing with their canines. In any case, they do need no less than an hour of strolling exercise every day. They additionally appreciate conveying things in their mouth as it gives them a significant assignment to be locked in with.

What Living with a Clumber Spaniel is Like

This variety is an incredible decision for families. Clumbers make durable, yet perky allies for kids. However long they get some every day work out, they can adjust to athletic proprietors or habitual slouches.

Tragically, medical issues abbreviate the Clumber's life, and they are not relied upon to live beyond 12 years, and may have intricacies from the get-go.

Care

Clumber Spaniels can do well in lofts or condominiums if their low to direct exercise necessities of a 20-to 30-minute day by day walk or recess are met.

All things considered, remember that they're basically an enormous canine. In the event that you live in a fifth-floor walkup, can you convey your grown-up Clumber all over the steps when he becomes ill or too old to even think about climbing them? It's something worth talking about to ponder.

By and large, Clumbers are peaceful and are not known as a variety that barks a ton. A fenced yard guards them from misfortune or burglary.

Other than strolls, Clumbers appreciate playing bring. At the point when they're pups, be that as it may, confine any running on hard surfaces or hopping on and off furnishings or sliding around on smooth floors and colliding with the divider. Those exercises can harm their as yet creating joints. Your Clumber little guy will pursue a ball however long you'll let him, regardless of whether he's drained, so it's dependent upon you to restrict his movement. Offer him a reprieve after the fifth bring or thereabouts.

Case preparing is a brilliant instrument to help in house preparing, and a case likewise gives a place of refuge to your Clumber Spaniel when you are no more. Clumbers are known for their capacity to get into things, even as grown-ups, so this guarantees that both your canine and your assets are protected when you are away.

A few Clumbers are inclined to colitis, irritation of the enormous entrail. On the off chance that your Clumber has delicate stools that contain spots of blood or bodily fluid yet in any case seems solid, he might have colitis.

Put him on a 24-hour quick, ensure he approaches a lot of water, then, at that point, give him tasteless suppers like chicken and rice for the following a few days. Step by step once again introduce his typical eating routine. If colitis repeats oftentimes, get some information about giving your Clumber an eating routine planned for canines with touchy stomach related frameworks.

Shedding and Grooming

Spaniels' tasty locks accompany a cost. They're high shedding and require some particular prepping strategies to stay satisfactory.

Brush the hair one time per week or so to keep away from tangles. Trim and wash depending on the situation. Take additional consideration to clean the Clumber's kinks of skin with a clammy fabric and dry them completely. This will assist with keeping away from an awful stench and disease.

The Clumber is especially vulnerable to ear contamination. To stay away from this, cut his hair back from the ears, and keep the trenches liberated from soil and trash.

CHAPTER FIVE

Feeding

Suggested every day sum: 2 to 2.5 cups of top notch dry food daily, isolated into two suppers. Little dogs might eat as much as 4 to 6 cups every day.

NOTE: How much your grown-up canine eats relies upon his size, age, construct, digestion, and action level. Canines are people, very much like individuals, and they don't all need a similar measure of food. It nearly should be obvious that an exceptionally dynamic canine will require in excess of a habitual slouch canine. The nature of canine food you purchase additionally has an effect — the better the canine food, the further it will go toward sustaining your canine and the less of it you'll have to shake into your canine's bowl.

In case you're uncertain whether he's overweight, give him the active test. Spot your hands on his back, thumbs along the spine and the fingers spread descending. You ought to have the option to feel yet not see his ribs. If you can't feel the ribs, he wants less food and a more drawn out walk.

For additional on taking care of your Clumber, see our rules for purchasing the right food, taking care of your pup, and taking care of your grown-up canine. •

Coat Tone And Preparing

The Clumber Spaniel has a delicate, medium-length coat that is thick and straight, lying level on the body. The ears, legs, and stomach have moderate padding — a more drawn out edge of hair — and there's a decoration underneath the neck, longer hair that is some of the time alluded to as a cover. Clumbers are not difficult to get ready for the show ring since they should look normal, with no shaving or managing but to clean the feet, back legs, and tail.

Their bodies are essentially white, as a rule with lemon or orange markings around the eyes and on the head or ears. Here and there they have spots on their gag — the space of the head before the eyes — and on the legs, body, and at the foundation of the tail. Clumbers who will be show canines ought to have as couple of markings on the body as could be expected, yet spots and markings on the body don't influence their capacity to be a family companion.

Clumber Spaniels are viewed as normal to substantial shedders, and there will be days when maybe it's snowing Clumber hair in your home. Day by day brushing is an unquestionable requirement to downplay free hair. Other than that, you definitely should simply manage the hair on their back legs and tail and between the stack of the feet to keep them looking perfect. Ask a reproducer or custodian to show you how.

A Clumber Spaniel's white coat can hold a lot of soil and trash, so go ahead and wash him as regularly as you might suspect vital. However long you're utilizing a cleanser made for canines, normal showers will not influence his jacket but to make it look perfect rather than grimy. Simply make certain to wash completely to keep irritation from cleanser buildup.

Start acclimating your Clumber to being brushed and inspected when he's a doggy. Handle his paws habitually — canines are sensitive with regards to their feet — and look inside his mouth and ears. Make prepping a positive encounter loaded up with commendation and remunerates, and you'll lay the foundation for simple veterinary tests and other taking care of when he's a grown-up.

As you groom, check for wounds, rashes, or indications of disease like redness, delicacy, or irritation on the skin, in the ears, nose, mouth, and eyes, and on the feet. Your cautious week after week test will assist you with spotting potential medical issues early.

The Clumber Spaniel is inclined to ear contaminations, so preventive consideration is significant. This can be pretty much as basic as drying your canine's ears in the wake of swimming and checking the ears routinely for indications of disease like a terrible stench, redness, or delicacy.

The Clumber with an ear disease may likewise shake his head regularly or scratch at his ears. Delicately clear out the ear — just the part you can see — with a cotton ball soaked with a cleaning arrangement suggested by your veterinarian. Never stick q-tips or whatever else into the ear waterway or you may harm it.

Clean your Clumber's teeth no less than a few times each week to eliminate tartar development and the microorganisms that hide inside it. Every day brushing is far better assuming you need to forestall gum infection and awful breath.

Trim nails consistently if your canine doesn't wear them out normally. If you can hear them tapping on the floor, they're excessively long. Short, flawlessly managed nails hold your legs back

from getting scratched when your
Clumber excitedly hops up to
welcome you.

• Children And Different Pets

It's been said that Clumbers and
children go together like frozen
yogurt and cake. Clumbers for the
most part love kids, particularly
kids who toss a ball for them to
get. They are typically defensive of
youngsters in the family and are
bound to leave than to snap or
snarl in case they're standing out
enough to be noticed from a kid.

In the event that your Clumber doggy is raised with your little child, you'll presumably see a wonderful kinship bloom. The baby may incidentally get smoothed on occasion by an extravagant youthful Clumber, however he'll be licked until he's in a good place again.

Regardless, canines are people, actually like individuals. Only one out of every odd Clumber who is brought up with children will take to them, particularly if the children are ineffectively acted. Grown-up Clumbers who haven't been raised with children might do best in families with more seasoned youngsters who see how to connect with canines.

A few Clumbers might be hesitant around kids they don't have a clue, and like most canines, they don't care for being charged by minuscule babies — or any other person. Shield your canine from these attacks, and show the kids you experience how to move toward a canine securely.

Continuously direct any communications among canines and small kids to forestall any gnawing or ear or tail pulling with respect to one or the other party. Show your youngster never to move toward any canine while he's eating or to attempt to remove the canine's food. No canine ought to at any point be left solo with a kid.

Clumber Spaniels likewise do very well with different canines and creatures, particularly in case they are raised with them. They are birdy, be that as it may, and you ought to ensure pet birds until you're certain your Clumber comprehends they're untouchable.

Young doggies

Clumber Spaniel young doggies are exceptionally dynamic and will cavort around cheerfully generally of the day. Their preparation should start early and they ought to be associated with different canines and people as right on time as could be expected.

THE END

Printed in Great Britain
by Amazon

83590289R00031